D1706881

To

Sabrina & Marco

From

_Me._

Date

_9/21/08_

Promises from God for Parents

© 2008 Christian Art Gifts, RSA
      Christian Art Gifts Inc., IL, USA

Compiled by Cornél de Klerk and Kylie Munger

Designed by Christian Art Gifts

Scripture quotations marked NIV are taken from the *Holy Bible*, New International Version®. NIV®. Copyright © 1973, 1978, 1984 by International Bible Society. Used by permission of Zondervan Publishing House. All rights reserved.

Scripture quotations marked NLT are taken from the *Holy Bible*, New Living Translation, copyright © 1996. Used by permission of Tyndale House Publishers, Inc., Carol Stream, Illinois 60188. All rights reserved.

Scripture quotations marked NKJV are taken from the *Holy Bible*, New King James Version. Copyright © 1979, 1980, 1982 by Thomas Nelson Publishers, Inc. Used by permission. All rights reserved.

Scripture quotations marked ESV are from the *Holy Bible*, English Standard Version, copyright © 2001 by Crossway Bibles, a division of Good News Publishers. Used by permission. All rights reserved.

Printed in China

ISBN 978-1-86920-970-4 – Pink
      978-1-86920-971-1 – Blue

08 09 10 11 12 13 14 15 16 17 – 10 9 8 7 6 5 4 3 2 1

PROMISES
FROM GOD
FOR
Parents

christian
art gifts.

Contents

Promises from God for Parents

1. When We Need ...

2. How to Deal with ...

6. For Developing a Christlike Spirit ...

Introduction

Train up a child in the way he should go; even when he is old he will not depart from it.

PROVERBS 22:6 ESV

Parenthood is a precious and sacred calling. It is also the most rewarding, and at the same time, demanding and challenging role we can fill.

As parents we need guidance, reassurance, strength, encouragement and direction all the time. *Promises from God for Parents* is filled with God's promises to encourage and reassure parents.

It will guide and direct them, equipping them for the special task of parenthood.

Acceptance

You are a people holy to the LORD your God. The LORD your God has chosen you out of all the peoples on the face of the earth to be His people, His treasured possession.

DEUTERONOMY 7:6 NIV

Know that the LORD, He is God; it is He who has made us, and not we ourselves; we are His people and the sheep of His pasture.

PSALM 100:3 NKJV

"Those the Father has given Me will come to Me, and I will never reject them. For I have come down from heaven to do the will of God who sent Me, not to do what I want."

JOHN 6:37-38 NLT

"I tell you the truth, whoever accepts anyone I send accepts Me; and whoever accepts Me accepts the One who sent Me."

JOHN 13:20 NIV

While we live, we live to please the Lord. And when we die, we go to be with the Lord. So in life and in death, we belong to the Lord. Christ died and rose again for this very purpose, so that He might be Lord of those who are alive and of those who have died.

ROMANS 14:8-9 NLT

Accept one another, then, just as Christ accepted you, in order to bring praise to God.

ROMANS 15:7 NIV

The LORD has appeared of old to me, saying: "Yes, I have loved you with an everlasting love; therefore with lovingkindness I have drawn you."

JEREMIAH 31:3 NKJV

For we are His workmanship, created in Christ Jesus for good works, which God prepared beforehand, that we should walk in them.

EPHESIANS 2:10 ESV

It is God who establishes us with you in Christ, and has anointed us, and who has also put His seal on us and given us His Spirit in our hearts as a guarantee.

2 CORINTHIANS 1:21-22 ESV

Now, thus says the LORD, who created you, O Jacob, and He who formed you, O Israel: "Fear not, for I have redeemed you; I have called you by your name; you are Mine."

ISAIAH 43:1 NKJV

"If you forgive men when they sin against you, your heavenly Father will also forgive you."

MATTHEW 6:14 NIV

Truly I understand that God shows no partiality, but in every nation anyone who fears Him and does what is right is acceptable to Him.

ACTS 10:34 ESV

Anger

"In your anger do not sin": Do not let the sun go down while you are still angry.

EPHESIANS 4:26 NIV

Whatever is true, whatever is honorable, whatever is just, whatever is pure, whatever is lovely, whatever is commendable, if there is any excellence, if there is anything worthy of praise, think about these things.

PHILIPPIANS 4:8 ESV

Refrain from anger and turn from wrath; do not fret – it leads only to evil.

PSALM 37:8 NIV

Those who control their anger have great understanding; those with a hasty temper will make mistakes.

PROVERBS 14:29 NLT

Dear friends, be quick to listen, slow to speak, and slow to get angry. Your anger can never make things right in God's sight.

JAMES 1:19-20 NLT

The LORD is compassionate and gracious, slow to anger, abounding in love. He does not treat us as our sins deserve or repay us according to our iniquities.

PSALM 103:8, 10 NIV

If possible, so far as it depends on you, live peaceably with all.

ROMANS 12:18 ESV

A gentle answer turns away wrath, but harsh words stir up anger.

PROVERBS 15:1 NLT

Now you yourselves are to put off all these: anger, wrath, malice, blasphemy, filthy language out of your mouth.

COLOSSIANS 3:8 NKJV

Kind words are like honey – sweet to the soul and healthy for the body.

PROVERBS 16:24 NLT

Better a patient man than a warrior, a man who controls his temper than one who takes a city.

PROVERBS 16:32 NIV

Keep away from angry, short-tempered people, or you will learn to be like them and endanger your soul.

PROVERBS 22:24-25 NLT

Let all bitterness and wrath and anger and clamor and slander be put away from you, along with all malice. Be kind to one another.

EPHESIANS 4:31-32 ESV

Anxiety

"Do not let your hearts be troubled. Trust in God; trust also in Me."

JOHN 14:1 NIV

"Which of you by being anxious can add a single hour to his span of life? If then you are not able to do as small a thing as that, why are you anxious about the rest? Seek His kingdom, and these things will be added to you."

LUKE 12:25-26, 31 ESV

For the eyes of the Lord are on the righteous, and His ears are open to their prayers.

1 PETER 3:12 NKJV

"Have I not commanded you? Be strong and courageous. Do not be terrified; do not be discouraged, for the LORD your God will be with you wherever you go."

JOSHUA 1:9 NIV

Humble yourselves under the mighty hand of God, that He may exalt you in due time, casting all your care upon Him, for He cares for you.

1 PETER 5:6-7 NKJV

"Come to Me, all of you who are weary and carry heavy burdens, and I will give you rest."

MATTHEW 11:28 NLT

An anxious heart weighs a man down, but a kind word cheers him up.

PROVERBS 12:25 NIV

Don't worry about anything; instead, pray about everything. Tell God what you need, and thank Him for all He has done. If you do this, you will experience God's peace, which is far more wonderful than the human mind can understand. His peace will guard your hearts and minds as you live in Christ Jesus.

PHILIPPIANS 4:6-7 NLT

Cast your burden on the LORD, and He will sustain you; He will never permit the righteous to be moved.

PSALM 55:22 ESV

Commit everything you do to the LORD. Trust Him, and He will help you.

PSALM 37:5 NLT

Say to those who are fearful-hearted, "Be strong, do not fear! Behold, your God will come with vengeance, with the recompense of God; He will come and save you."

ISAIAH 35:4 NKJV

Search me, O God, and know my heart; test me and know my anxious thoughts. See if there is any offensive way in me, and lead me in the way everlasting.

PSALM 139:23-24 NIV

Blessings

Blessed are those who trust in the LORD and have made the LORD their hope and confidence.

JEREMIAH 17:7 NLT

The blessing of the LORD makes one rich, and He adds no sorrow with it.

PROVERBS 10:22 NKJV

The LORD bless you and keep you; the LORD make His face to shine upon you and be gracious to you; the LORD lift up His countenance upon you and give you peace.

NUMBERS 6:24-26 ESV

The LORD will give strength to His people; the LORD will bless His people with peace.

PSALM 29:11 NKJV

Don't repay evil for evil. Don't retaliate when people say unkind things about you. Instead, pay them back with a blessing. That is what God wants you to do, and He will bless you for it.

1 PETER 3:9 NLT

Taste and see that the LORD is good; blessed is the man who takes refuge in Him.

PSALM 34:8 NIV

Blessed is the man who does not walk in the counsel of the wicked or stand in the way of sinners or sit in the seat of mockers. But his delight is in the law of the LORD, and on His law he meditates day and night.

PSALM 1:1-2 NIV

God is able to provide you with every blessing in abundance, so that having all sufficiency in all things at all times, you may abound in every good work.

2 CORINTHIANS 9:8 ESV

The righteous man leads a blameless life; blessed are his children after him.

PROVERBS 20:7 NIV

For You, O LORD, will bless the righteous; with favor You will surround him as with a shield.

PSALM 5:12 NKJV

Blessed is the man who makes the LORD his trust.

PSALM 40:4 ESV

Blessed is he who has regard for the weak; the LORD delivers him in times of trouble.

PSALM 41:1 NIV

May God be merciful and bless us. May His face shine with favor upon us.

PSALM 67:1-2 NLT

Children

Behold, children are a heritage from the LORD, the fruit of the womb a reward. Like arrows in the hand of a warrior are the children of one's youth. Blessed is the man who fills his quiver with them!

PSALM 127:3-5 ESV

Grandchildren are the crowning glory of the aged; parents are the pride of their children.

PROVERBS 17:6 NLT

Even a child is known by his actions, by whether his conduct is pure and right.

PROVERBS 20:11 NIV

If you refuse to discipline your children, it proves you don't love them; if you love your children, you will be prompt to discipline them.

PROVERBS 13:24 NLT

Children, obey your parents in the Lord, for this is right.

EPHESIANS 6:1 ESV

He took a little child and set him in the midst of them. And when He had taken him in His arms, He said to them, "Whoever receives one of these little children in My name receives Me; and whoever receives Me, receives not Me but Him who sent Me."

MARK 9:36-37 NKJV

Happy are those who fear the LORD. Yes, happy are those who delight in doing what He commands. Their children will be successful everywhere; an entire generation of godly people will be blessed.

PSALM 112:1-2 NLT

All your children shall be taught by the LORD, and great shall be the peace of your children.

ISAIAH 54:13 ESV

Watch out! Be very careful never to forget what you have seen the LORD do for you. Do not let these things escape from your mind as long as you live! And be sure to pass them on to your children and grandchildren.

DEUTERONOMY 4:9 NLT

Fathers, do not provoke your children to anger, but bring them up in the discipline and instruction of the Lord.

EPHESIANS 6:4 ESV

Train up a child in the way he should go, and when he is old he will not depart from it.

PROVERBS 22:6 NKJV

Come, my children, listen to me; I will teach you the fear of the LORD.

PSALM 34:11 NIV

Commitment

Commit your way to the LORD, trust also in Him, and He shall bring it to pass. He shall bring forth your righteousness as the light, and your justice as the noonday.

PSALM 37:5-6 NKJV

I press on to take hold of that for which Christ Jesus took hold of me. Brothers, I do not consider myself yet to have taken hold of it. But one thing I do: Forgetting what is behind and straining toward what is ahead, I press on toward the goal to win the prize for which God has called me heavenward in Christ Jesus.

PHILIPPIANS 3:12-14 NIV

Let your heart therefore be wholly true to the LORD our God, walking in His statutes and keeping His commandments.

1 KINGS 8:61 ESV

Into Your hand I commit my spirit; You have redeemed me, O LORD God of truth.

PSALM 31:5 NKJV

Commit your work to the LORD, and then your plans will succeed.

PROVERBS 16:3 NLT

So then, just as you received Christ Jesus as Lord, continue to live in Him, rooted and built up in Him, strengthened in the faith as you were taught, and overflowing with thankfulness.

COLOSSIANS 2:6-7 NIV

Don't get tired of doing what is good. Don't get discouraged and give up, for we will reap a harvest of blessing at the appropriate time.

GALATIANS 6:9 NLT

Let those who suffer according to God's will entrust their souls to a faithful Creator while doing good.

1 PETER 4:19 ESV

When the storm has swept by, the wicked are gone, but the righteous stand firm forever.

PROVERBS 10:25 NIV

Therefore, brethren, stand fast and hold the traditions which you were taught, whether by word or our epistle. Now may our Lord Jesus Christ Himself, who has loved us and given us everlasting consolation and good hope by grace, comfort your hearts and establish you in every good word and work.

2 THESSALONIANS 2:15-17 NKJV

Do not offer the parts of your body to sin, as instruments of wickedness, but rather offer yourselves to God, as those who have been brought from death to life; and offer the parts of your body to Him as instruments of righteousness.

ROMANS 6:13 NIV

If you are not firm in faith, you will not be firm at all.

ISAIAH 7:9 ESV

Conflict

Be completely humble and gentle; be patient, bearing with one another in love.

EPHESIANS 4:2 NIV

Now, dear brothers and sisters, I appeal to you by the authority of the Lord Jesus Christ to stop arguing among yourselves. Let there be real harmony so there won't be divisions in the church. I plead with you to be of one mind, united in thought and purpose.

1 CORINTHIANS 1:10 NLT

Behold, how good and how pleasant it is for brethren to dwell together in unity!

PSALM 133:1 NKJV

See that no one repays anyone evil for evil, but always seek to do good to one another and to everyone.

1 THESSALONIANS 5:15 ESV

May the God who gives endurance and encouragement give you a spirit of unity among yourselves as you follow Christ Jesus, so that with one heart and mouth you may glorify the God and Father of our Lord Jesus Christ.

ROMANS 15:5-6 NIV

Don't grumble about each other, my brothers and sisters, or God will judge you. For look! The great Judge is coming. He is standing at the door!

JAMES 5:9 NLT

Remind the people to be subject to rulers and authorities, to be obedient, to be ready to do whatever is good, to slander no one, to be peaceable and considerate, and to show true humility toward all men.

TITUS 3:1-2 NIV

Always keep yourselves united in the Holy Spirit, and bind yourselves together with peace.

EPHESIANS 4:3 NLT

The Lord's servant must not be quarrelsome but kind to everyone, able to teach, correcting his opponents with gentleness.

2 TIMOTHY 2:24-25 ESV

Therefore, as the elect of God, holy and beloved, put on tender mercies, kindness, humility, meekness, longsuffering; bearing with one another, and forgiving one another.

COLOSSIANS 3:12-13 NKJV

"God blesses those who work for peace, for they will be called the children of God."

MATTHEW 5:9 NLT

Above all these put on love, which binds everything together in perfect harmony.

COLOSSIANS 3:14 ESV

Criticism

If you are insulted because of the name of Christ, you are blessed, for the Spirit of glory and of God rests on you.

1 PETER 4:14 NIV

"Blessed are you when others revile you and persecute you and utter all kinds of evil against you falsely on My account. Rejoice and be glad, for your reward is great in heaven."

MATTHEW 5:11-12 ESV

A fool is quick-tempered, but a wise person stays calm when insulted.

PROVERBS 12:16 NLT

Rejoice that you participate in the sufferings of Christ, so that you may be overjoyed when His glory is revealed.

1 PETER 4:13 NIV

Why do you judge your brother? Or why do you show contempt for your brother? For we shall all stand before the judgment seat of Christ.

ROMANS 14:10 NKJV

The ear that listens to life-giving reproof will dwell among the wise.

PROVERBS 15:31 ESV

Some people make cutting remarks, but the words of the wise bring healing.

PROVERBS 12:18 NLT

It is better to hear the rebuke of the wise than for a man to hear the song of fools.

ECCLESIASTES 7:5 NKJV

"Pray for the happiness of those who curse you. Pray for those who hurt you. If someone slaps you on one cheek, turn the other cheek."

LUKE 6:28-29 NLT

Don't speak evil against each other, my dear brothers and sisters. If you criticize each other, then you are criticizing and condemning God's law.

JAMES 4:11 NLT

"Judge not, that you be not judged. For with what judgment you judge, you will be judged; and with the measure you use, it will be measured back to you."

MATTHEW 7:1-2 NKJV

"Let those who have never sinned throw the first stones!"

JOHN 8:7 NLT

Judge nothing before the appointed time; wait till the Lord comes. He will bring to light what is hidden in darkness and will expose the motives of men's hearts. At that time each will receive his praise from God.

1 CORINTHIANS 4:5 NIV

Discipline

My son, do not make light of the Lord's discipline, and do not lose heart when He rebukes you, because the Lord disciplines those He loves, and He punishes everyone He accepts as a son.

HEBREWS 12:5-6 NIV

Behold, blessed is the one whom God reproves; therefore despise not the discipline of the Almighty.

JOB 5:17 ESV

No discipline is enjoyable while it is happening – it is painful! But afterward there will be a quiet harvest of right living for those who are trained in this way.

HEBREWS 12:11 NLT

Discipline your son, for in that there is hope; do not be a willing party to his death.

PROVERBS 19:18 NIV

Discipline your son, and he will give you rest; he will give delight to your heart.

PROVERBS 29:17 ESV

Listen, my son, to your father's instruction and do not forsake your mother's teaching.

PROVERBS 1:8 NIV

So you should realize that just as a parent disciplines a child, the LORD your God disciplines you to help you. So obey the commands of the LORD your God by walking in His ways and fearing Him.

DEUTERONOMY 8:5-6 NLT

Whoever heeds instruction is on the path to life, but he who rejects reproof leads others astray.

PROVERBS 10:17 ESV

To learn, you must love discipline; it is stupid to hate correction.

PROVERBS 12:1 NLT

Blessed is the man whom You discipline, O
LORD, and whom You teach out of Your law.

PSALM 94:12 ESV

For whom the LORD loves He corrects, just as a
father the son in whom he delights.

PROVERBS 3:12 NKJV

It is better for a man to hear the rebuke of the
wise than to hear the song of fools.

ECCLESIASTES 7:5 ESV

A wise child accepts a parent's discipline; a young
mocker refuses to listen.

PROVERBS 13:1 NLT

Hold on to instruction, do not let it go; guard it
well, for it is your life.

PROVERBS 4:13 NIV

Encouragement

Be strong and courageous. Do not be terrified; do not be discouraged, for the LORD your God will be with you wherever you go.

JOSHUA 1:9 NIV

Cast your burden on the LORD, and He will sustain you; He will never permit the righteous to be moved.

PSALM 55:22 ESV

If we are faithful to the end, trusting God just as firmly as when we first believed, we will share in all that belongs to Christ.

HEBREWS 3:14 NLT

It is God who arms me with strength, and makes my way perfect. He makes my feet like the feet of deer, and sets me on my high places.

PSALM 18:32-33 NKJV

Though I walk in the midst of trouble, You preserve my life. The LORD will fulfill His purpose for me; Your love, O LORD, endures forever – do not abandon the works of Your hands.

PSALM 138:7-8 NIV

Do not be afraid! The LORD your God will go ahead of you. He will neither fail you nor forsake you.

DEUTERONOMY 31:6 NLT

If the LORD delights in a man's way, He makes his steps firm; though he stumble, he will not fall, for the LORD upholds him with His hand.

PSALM 37:23-24 NIV

The love of the LORD remains forever with those who fear Him. His salvation extends to the children's children of those who are faithful to His covenant, of those who obey His commandments!

PSALM 103:17-18 NLT

Commit your way to the LORD, trust in Him, and He will act.

PSALM 37:5 ESV

May our Lord Jesus Christ and God our Father, who loved us and in His special favor gave us everlasting comfort and good hope, comfort your hearts and give you strength in every good thing you do and say.

2 THESSALONIANS 2:16-17 NLT

Be strong and do not let your hands be weak, for your work shall be rewarded!

2 CHRONICLES 15:7 NKJV

I can do everything through Him who gives me strength.

PHILIPPIANS 4:13 NIV

*F*aith

"Have faith in God," Jesus answered. "I tell you the truth, if anyone says to this mountain, 'Go, throw yourself into the sea,' and does not doubt in his heart but believes that what he says will happen, it will be done for him."

MARK 11:22-23 NIV

Believe in the LORD your God, and you will be able to stand firm.

2 CHRONICLES 20:20 NLT

Who is it that overcomes the world? Only he who believes that Jesus is the Son of God.

1 JOHN 5:5 NIV

It is impossible to please God without faith. Anyone who wants to come to Him must believe that there is a God and that He rewards those who sincerely seek Him.

HEBREWS 11:6 NLT

If any of you lacks wisdom, let him ask of God, who gives to all liberally, and it will be given to him. But let him ask in faith, with no doubting, for he who doubts is like a wave of the sea driven and tossed by the wind.

JAMES 1:5-6 NKJV

Though you have not seen Him, you love Him. Though you do not now see Him, you believe in Him and rejoice with joy that is inexpressible and filled with glory, obtaining the outcome of your faith, the salvation of your souls.

1 PETER 1:8-9 ESV

We walk by faith, not by sight.

2 CORINTHIANS 5:7 NKJV

Then Jesus told him, "You believe because you have seen Me. Blessed are those who haven't seen Me and believe anyway."

JOHN 20:29 NLT

"I tell you, whatever you ask in prayer, believe that you have received it, and it will be yours."

MARK 11:24 ESV

Since we have been justified through faith, we have peace with God through our Lord Jesus Christ, through whom we have gained access by faith into this grace in which we now stand. And we rejoice in the hope of the glory of God.

ROMANS 5:1-2 NIV

"I assure you, anyone who believes in Me already has eternal life."

JOHN 6:47 NLT

Now faith is the assurance of things hoped for, the conviction of things not seen.

HEBREWS 11:1 ESV

Family

As for me and my house, we will serve the LORD.

JOSHUA 24:15 NKJV

"Honor your father and mother. Then you will live a long, full life in the land the LORD your God will give you."

EXODUS 20:12 NLT

If someone says, "I love God," and hates his brother, he is a liar; for he who does not love his brother whom he has seen, how can he love God whom he has not seen? And this commandment we have from Him: that he who loves God must love his brother also.

1 JOHN 4:20-21 NKJV

You are all sons of God through faith in Christ Jesus, for all of you who were baptized into Christ have clothed yourselves with Christ.

GALATIANS 3:26-27 NIV

All of you be of one mind, having compassion for one another, love as brothers, be tenderhearted, be courteous.

1 PETER 3:8 NKJV

As a father has compassion on his children, so the LORD has compassion on those who fear Him.

PSALM 103:13 NIV

In God's goodness He chose to make us His own children by giving us His true word. And we, out of all creation, became His choice possession.

JAMES 1:18 NLT

"These commandments that I give you today are to be upon your hearts. Impress them on your children. Talk about them when you sit at home and when you walk along the road, when you lie down and when you get up."

DEUTERONOMY 6:6-7 NIV

"I will be a Father to you, and you will be My sons and daughters," says the Lord Almighty.

2 CORINTHIANS 6:18 NIV

Behold what manner of love the Father has bestowed on us, that we should be called children of God!

1 JOHN 3:1 NKJV

For all who are led by the Spirit of God are sons of God.

ROMANS 8:14 ESV

You are no longer foreigners and aliens, but fellow citizens with God's people and members of God's household, built on the foundation of the apostles and prophets, with Christ Jesus Himself as the chief cornerstone.

EPHESIANS 2:19-20 NIV

Finances

As for every man to whom God has given riches and wealth, and given him power to eat of it, to receive his heritage and rejoice in his labor – this is the gift of God.

ECCLESIASTES 5:19 NKJV

"Bring the whole tithe into the storehouse, that there may be food in My house. Test Me in this," says the LORD Almighty, "and see if I will not throw open the floodgates of heaven and pour out so much blessing that you will not have room enough for it."

MALACHI 3:10 NIV

The LORD is my shepherd; I have everything I need.

PSALM 23:1 NLT

God will supply every need of yours according to His riches in glory in Christ Jesus.

PHILIPPIANS 4:19 ESV

God will generously provide all you need. Then you will always have everything you need and plenty left over to share with others.

2 CORINTHIANS 9:8 NLT

I know what it is to be in need, and I know what it is to have plenty. I have learned the secret of being content in any and every situation, whether well fed or hungry, whether living in plenty or in want. I can do everything through Him who gives me strength.

PHILIPPIANS 4:12-13 NIV

Let your conduct be without covetousness; be content with such things as you have. For He Himself has said, "I will never leave you nor forsake you." So we may boldly say: "The LORD is my helper; I will not fear. What can man do to me?"

HEBREWS 13:5-6 NKJV

"Give, and it will be given to you. A good measure, pressed down, shaken together and running over, will be poured into your lap."

LUKE 6:38 NIV

"Don't worry about everyday life – whether you have enough food, drink, and clothes. Doesn't life consist of more than food and clothing? And if God cares so wonderfully for flowers that are here today and gone tomorrow, won't He more surely care for you? You have so little faith!"

MATTHEW 6:25, 30 NLT

"Do not lay up for yourselves treasures on earth, where moth and rust destroy and where thieves break in and steal; but lay up for yourselves treasures in heaven, where neither moth nor rust destroys and where thieves do not break in and steal. For where your treasure is, there your heart will be also."

MATTHEW 6:19-21 NKJV

Godly people give generously to the poor. Their good deeds will never be forgotten.

2 CORINTHIANS 9:9 NLT

"Watch out! Be on your guard against all kinds of greed; a man's life does not consist in the abundance of his possessions."

LUKE 12:15 NIV

Forgiveness

If we confess our sins, He is faithful and just to forgive us our sins and to cleanse us from all unrighteousness.

1 JOHN 1:9 ESV

"If My people who are called by My name will humble themselves, and pray and seek My face, and turn from their wicked ways, then I will hear from heaven, and will forgive their sin and heal their land."

2 CHRONICLES 7:14 NKJV

You forgave the iniquity of Your people; You covered all their sin.

PSALM 85:2 ESV

"Though your sins are like scarlet, they shall be as white as snow; though they are red as crimson, they shall be like wool."

ISAIAH 1:18 NIV

"I am He who blots out your transgressions for My own sake; and I will not remember your sins."

ISAIAH 43:25 NKJV

He has removed our rebellious acts as far away from us as the east is from the west.

PSALM 103:12 NLT

I acknowledged my sin to You, and I did not cover my iniquity; I said, "I will confess my transgressions to the LORD," and You forgave the iniquity of my sin.

PSALM 32:5 ESV

"I assure you that any sin can be forgiven."

MARK 3:28 NLT

"I tell you: Love your enemies and pray for those who persecute you, that you may be sons of your Father in heaven. He causes His sun to rise on the evil and the good, and sends rain on the righteous and the unrighteous."

MATTHEW 5:44-45 NIV

You must make allowance for each other's faults and forgive the person who offends you. Remember, the Lord forgave you, so you must forgive others.

COLOSSIANS 3:13 NLT

"For if you forgive men their trespasses, your heavenly Father will also forgive you. But if you do not forgive men their trespasses, neither will your Father forgive your trespasses."

MATTHEW 6:14-15 NKJV

"When you stand praying, if you hold anything against anyone, forgive him, so that your Father in heaven may forgive you your sins."

MARK 11:25 NIV

"If another believer sins, rebuke him; then if he repents, forgive him. Even if he wrongs you seven times a day and each time turns again and asks forgiveness, forgive him."

LUKE 17:3-4 NLT

God's Will

Trust in the LORD with all your heart and lean not on your own understanding; in all your ways acknowledge Him, and He will make your paths straight.

PROVERBS 3:5-6 NIV

It is God who works in you both to will and to do for His good pleasure.

PHILIPPIANS 2:13 NKJV

If you are suffering according to God's will, keep on doing what is right, and trust yourself to the God who made you, for He will never fail you.

1 PETER 4:19 NLT

Do not be conformed to this world, but be transformed by the renewing of your mind, that you may prove what is that good and acceptable and perfect will of God.

ROMANS 12:2 NKJV

He has showed you, O man, what is good. And what does the LORD require of you? To act justly and to love mercy and to walk humbly with your God.

MICAH 6:8 NIV

Jesus said to the people who believed in Him, "You are truly My disciples if you keep obeying My teachings. And you will know the truth, and the truth will set you free."

JOHN 8:31-32 NLT

Give thanks in all circumstances; for this is the will of God in Christ Jesus for you.

1 THESSALONIANS 5:18 ESV

If you call out for insight and cry aloud for understanding, and if you look for it as for silver and search for it as for hidden treasure, then you will understand the fear of the LORD and find the knowledge of God.

PROVERBS 2:3-5 NIV

"If anyone's will is to do God's will, he will know whether the teaching is from God or whether I am speaking on My own authority."

JOHN 7:17 ESV

You need to persevere so that when you have done the will of God, you will receive what He has promised.

HEBREWS 10:36 NIV

Don't copy the behavior and customs of this world, but let God transform you into a new person by changing the way you think. Then you will know what God wants you to do, and you will know how good and pleasing and perfect His will really is.

ROMANS 12:2 NLT

He who searches our hearts knows the mind of the Spirit, because the Spirit intercedes for the saints in accordance with God's will.

ROMANS 8:27 NIV

Guidance

"When the Spirit of truth comes, He will guide you into all truth. He will tell you about the future."

JOHN 16:13 NLT

For You are my lamp, O LORD; the LORD shall enlighten my darkness.

2 SAMUEL 22:29 NKJV

"I will lead the blind by ways they have not known, along unfamiliar paths I will guide them; I will turn the darkness into light before them and make the rough places smooth. These are the things I will do; I will not forsake them."

ISAIAH 42:16 NIV

You will hear a voice say, "This is the way; turn around and walk here."

ISAIAH 30:21 NLT

The LORD will guide you continually and satisfy your desire in scorched places and make your bones strong; and you shall be like a watered garden, like a spring of water, whose waters do not fail.

ISAIAH 58:11 ESV

If you need wisdom – if you want to know what God wants you to do – ask Him, and He will gladly tell you.

JAMES 1:5 NLT

I will instruct you and teach you in the way you should go; I will counsel you and watch over you.

PSALM 32:8 NIV

"For I know the thoughts that I think toward you," says the LORD, "thoughts of peace and not of evil, to give you a future and a hope."

JEREMIAH 29:11 NKJV

You search out my path and my lying down and are acquainted with all my ways.

PSALM 139:3 ESV

A man's heart plans his way, but the LORD directs his steps.

PROVERBS 16:9 NKJV

All this comes from the LORD Almighty, wonderful in counsel and magnificent in wisdom.

ISAIAH 28:29 NIV

The steps of a good man are ordered by the LORD, and He delights in his way.

PSALM 37:23 NKJV

The LORD is good and does what is right; He shows the proper path to those who go astray. He leads the humble in what is right, teaching them His way.

PSALM 25:8-9 NLT

*H*ardships

The LORD is my light and my salvation; whom shall I fear? The LORD is the stronghold of my life; of whom shall I be afraid? Though an army encamp against me, my heart shall not fear; though war arise against me, yet I will be confident.

PSALM 27:1, 3 ESV

Look to the LORD and His strength; seek His face always. Remember the wonders He has done, His miracles, and the judgments He pronounced.

1 CHRONICLES 16:11-12 NIV

We know that for those who love God all things work together for good, for those who are called according to His purpose.

ROMANS 8:28 ESV

When I called, You answered me; You made me bold and stouthearted.

PSALM 138:3 NIV

You are a shield around me, O LORD; You bestow glory on me and lift up my head. To the LORD I cry aloud, and He answers me from His holy hill. I lie down and sleep; I wake again, because the LORD sustains me.

PSALM 3:3-5 NIV

Weeping may go on all night, but joy comes with the morning.

PSALM 30:5 NLT

Behold, He who keeps Israel will neither slumber nor sleep. The LORD is your keeper; the LORD is your shade on your right hand. The sun shall not strike you by day, nor the moon by night.

PSALM 121:4-6 ESV

We are pressed on every side by troubles, but we are not crushed and broken. We are perplexed, but we don't give up and quit. We get knocked down, but we get up again and keep going.

2 CORINTHIANS 4:8-9 NLT

Consider it pure joy, my brothers, whenever you face trials of many kinds, because you know that the testing of your faith develops perseverance.

JAMES 1:2-3 NIV

Those who live in the shelter of the Most High will find rest in the shadow of the Almighty.

PSALM 91:1 NLT

Why are you cast down, O my soul? And why are you disquieted within me? Hope in God; for I shall yet praise Him, the help of my countenance and my God.

PSALM 43:5 NKJV

Take courage! Do not let your hands be weak, for your work shall be rewarded.

2 CHRONICLES 15:7 ESV

Honesty

Light is shed upon the righteous and joy on the upright in heart.

PSALM 97:11 NIV

He who speaks truth declares righteousness, but a false witness, deceit.

PROVERBS 12:17 NKJV

Don't lie to each other, for you have stripped off your old evil nature and all its wicked deeds. In its place you have clothed yourselves with a brand-new nature that is continually being renewed as you learn more and more about Christ, who created this new nature within you.

COLOSSIANS 3:9-10 NLT

The LORD God is a sun and shield; the LORD will give grace and glory; no good thing will He withhold from those who walk uprightly.

PSALM 84:11 NKJV

Whatever is true, whatever is noble, whatever is right, whatever is pure, whatever is lovely, whatever is admirable – if anything is excellent or praiseworthy – think about such things.

PHILIPPIANS 4:8 NIV

Who may ascend into the hill of the LORD? Or who may stand in His holy place? He who has clean hands and a pure heart.

PSALM 24:3-4 NKJV

Good people are guided by their honesty; treacherous people are destroyed by their dishonesty.

PROVERBS 11:3 NLT

I know, my God, that You test the heart and are pleased with integrity. All these things have I given willingly and with honest intent.

1 CHRONICLES 29:17 NIV

Truth stands the test of time; lies are soon exposed.

PROVERBS 12:19 NLT

Light dawns in the darkness for the upright; He is gracious, merciful, and righteous.

PSALM 112:4 ESV

May God Himself, the God of peace, sanctify you through and through. May your whole spirit, soul and body be kept blameless at the coming of our Lord Jesus Christ. The One who calls you is faithful and He will do it.

1 THESSALONIANS 5:23-24 NIV

"As for that in the good soil, they are those who, hearing the word, hold it fast in an honest and good heart, and bear fruit with patience."

LUKE 8:15 ESV

You, O LORD, will bless the righteous; with favor You will surround him.

PSALM 5:12 NKJV

Hope

There are three things that will endure – faith, hope, and love.

1 CORINTHIANS 13:13 NLT

We who live by the Spirit eagerly wait to receive everything promised to us who are right with God through faith.

GALATIANS 5:5 NLT

May the God of hope fill you with all joy and peace in believing, that you may abound in hope by the power of the Holy Spirit.

ROMANS 15:13 NKJV

Those who fear You shall see me and rejoice, because I have hoped in Your word.

PSALM 119:74 ESV

For everything that was written in the past was written to teach us, so that through endurance and the encouragement of the Scriptures we might have hope.

ROMANS 15:4 NIV

Be strong and take courage, all you who put your hope in the LORD!

PSALM 31:24 NLT

The eyes of the LORD are on those who fear Him, on those whose hope is in His unfailing love.

PSALM 33:18 NIV

Let us hold fast the confession of our hope without wavering, for He who promised is faithful.

HEBREWS 10:23 NKJV

O Lord, You alone are my hope. I've trusted You, O LORD, from childhood.

PSALM 71:5 NLT

Let Your unfailing love surround us, LORD, for our hope is in You alone.

PSALM 33:22 NLT

The LORD is good to those whose hope is in Him, to the one who seeks Him.

LAMENTATIONS 3:25 NIV

Blessed is the man who trusts in the LORD, and whose hope is the LORD.

JEREMIAH 17:7 NKJV

Put your hope in the LORD, for with the LORD is unfailing love and redemption.

PSALM 130:7 NIV

I wait quietly before God, for my hope is in Him.

PSALM 62:5 NLV

Integrity

People with integrity have firm footing, but those who follow crooked paths will slip and fall.

PROVERBS 10:9 NLT

As for me, You uphold me in my integrity, and set me before Your face forever.

PSALM 41:12 NKJV

Let everything you do reflect the integrity and seriousness of your teaching. Let your teaching be so correct that it can't be criticized.

TITUS 2:7-8 NLT

He has told you what is good; and what does the LORD require of you but to do justice, and to love kindness, and to walk humbly with your God?

MICAH 6:8 ESV

Light is sown for the righteous, and joy for the upright in heart. Rejoice in the LORD and give thanks to His holy name!

PSALM 97:11-12 ESV

I know, my God, that You test the heart and are pleased with integrity.

1 CHRONICLES 29:17 NIV

Better is the poor who walks in his integrity than one who is perverse in his lips, and is a fool.

PROVERBS 19:1 NKJV

The LORD is righteous; He loves righteous deeds; the upright shall behold His face.

PSALM 11:7 ESV

Righteousness guards the man of integrity, but wickedness overthrows the sinner.

PROVERBS 13:6 NIV

For only the upright will live in the land, and those who have integrity will remain in it.

PROVERBS 2:21 NLT

The integrity of the upright guides them, but the unfaithful are destroyed by their duplicity.

PROVERBS 11:3 NIV

Whoever walks in integrity will be delivered, but he who is crooked in his ways will suddenly fall.

PROVERBS 28:18 ESV

May integrity and honesty protect me, for I put my hope in You.

PSALM 25:21 NLT

Lord, who may dwell in Your sanctuary? He whose walk is blameless and who does what is righteous, who speaks the truth from his heart.

PSALM 15:1-2 NIV

Joy

Be glad in the LORD and rejoice, you righteous; and shout for joy, all you upright in heart!

PSALM 32:11 NKJV

You have made known to me the path of life; You will fill me with joy in Your presence, with eternal pleasures at Your right hand.

PSALM 16:11 NIV

Always be joyful. Keep on praying. No matter what happens, always be thankful, for this is God's will for you who belong to Christ Jesus.

1 THESSALONIANS 5:16-18 NLT

"If you keep My commandments, you will abide in My love, just as I have kept My Father's commandments and abide in His love. These things I have spoken to you, that My joy may remain in you, and that your joy may be full."

JOHN 15:10-11 NKJV

The LORD your God will bless you in all your produce and in all the work of your hands, so that you will be altogether joyful.

DEUTERONOMY 16:15 ESV

You will go out in joy and be led forth in peace; the mountains and hills will burst into song before you, and all the trees of the field will clap their hands.

ISAIAH 55:12 NIV

Great is the LORD and most worthy of praise. Splendor and majesty are before Him; strength and joy in His dwelling place.

1 CHRONICLES 16:25, 27 NIV

Go and celebrate with a feast of choice foods and sweet drinks, and share gifts of food with people who have nothing prepared. This is a sacred day before our Lord. Don't be dejected and sad, for the joy of the LORD is your strength!

NEHEMIAH 8:10 NLT

Those who sow in tears will reap with songs of joy. He who goes out weeping, carrying seed to sow, will return with songs of joy, carrying sheaves with him.

PSALM 126:5-6 NIV

I am overwhelmed with joy in the LORD my God! For He has dressed me with the clothing of salvation and draped me in a robe of righteousness. I am like a bridegroom in his wedding suit or a bride with her jewels.

ISAIAH 61:10 NLT

My soul shall be satisfied as with marrow and fatness, and my mouth shall praise You with joyful lips. Because You have been my help, therefore in the shadow of Your wings I will rejoice.

PSALM 63:5, 7 NKJV

In Him our hearts rejoice, for we are trusting in His holy name.

PSALM 33:21 NLT

Listening

My child, listen to me and treasure my instructions. Then you will understand what is right, just, and fair.

PROVERBS 2:1, 9 NLT

The LORD will make you the head, not the tail. If you pay attention to the commands of the LORD your God that I give you this day and carefully follow them, you will always be at the top, never at the bottom.

DEUTERONOMY 28:13 NIV

Listen closely to everything I say. Be careful to obey. Then all will go well with you.

DEUTERONOMY 6:3 NLT

He who listens to reproof gains intelligence.

PROVERBS 15:32 ESV

"Listen to Me. I created you and have cared for you since before you were born. I will be your God throughout your lifetime."

ISAIAH 46:3-4 NLT

My voice You shall hear in the morning, O LORD; in the morning I will direct it to You, and I will look up.

PSALM 5:3 NKJV

We can be confident that He will listen to us whenever we ask Him for anything in line with His will.

1 JOHN 5:14 NLT

"Listen to Me. I am the first and I am the last. My own hand laid the foundations of the earth."

ISAIAH 48:12-13 NIV

"Blessed are those who hear the word of God and keep it!"

LUKE 11:28 NKJV

Let those who are wise understand these things. Let those who are discerning listen carefully. The paths of the LORD are true and right, and righteous people live by walking in them.

HOSEA 14:9 NLT

He who answers before listening – that is his folly and his shame.

PROVERBS 18:13 NIV

Come here and listen to me! I'll pour out the spirit of wisdom upon you and make you wise.

PROVERBS 1:23 NLT

Whoever listens to me will dwell safely, and will be secure, without fear of evil.

PROVERBS 1:33 NKJV

Do not merely listen to the word, and so deceive yourselves. Do what it says.

JAMES 1:23 NIV

Love each other deeply, because love covers over a multitude of sins.

1 PETER 4:8 NIV

Beloved, let us love one another, for love is from God, and whoever loves has been born of God and knows God. Anyone who does not love does not know God, because God is love.

1 JOHN 4:7-8 ESV

Eye has not seen, nor ear heard, nor have entered into the heart of man the things which God has prepared for those who love Him.

1 CORINTHIANS 2:9 NKJV

Live a life filled with love for others, following the example of Christ, who loved you and gave Himself as a sacrifice to take away your sins. And God was pleased, because that sacrifice was like sweet perfume to Him.

EPHESIANS 5:2 NLT

Love is patient, love is kind. It does not envy, it does not boast, it is not proud. It is not rude, it is not self-seeking, it is not easily angered, it keeps no record of wrongs. It always protects, always trusts, always hopes, always perseveres.

1 CORINTHIANS 13:4-5, 7 NIV

"A new commandment I give to you, that you love one another: just as I have loved you, you also are to love one another. By this all people will know that you are My disciples, if you have love for one another."

JOHN 13:34-35 ESV

The entire law is summed up in a single command: "Love your neighbor as yourself."

GALATIANS 5:14 NIV

Put on then, as God's chosen ones, holy and beloved, compassion, kindness, humility, meekness, and patience. And above all these put on love, which binds everything together in perfect harmony.

COLOSSIANS 3:12, 14 ESV

I pray that Christ will be more and more at home in your hearts as you trust in Him. May your roots go down deep into the soil of God's marvelous love. And may you have the power to understand how high, and how deep His love really is.

EPHESIANS 3:17-18 NLT

"I have loved you with an everlasting love; therefore I have continued My faithfulness to you."

JEREMIAH 31:3 ESV

For I am persuaded that neither death nor life, nor angels nor principalities nor powers, nor things present nor things to come, nor height nor depth, nor any other created thing, shall be able to separate us from the love of God which is in Christ Jesus our Lord.

ROMANS 8:38-39 NKJV

"For God so loved the world that He gave His one and only Son, that whoever believes in Him shall not perish but have eternal life."

JOHN 3:16 NIV

Kindness

"Do for others what you would like them to do for you. This is a summary of all that is taught in the law and the prophets."

MATTHEW 7:12 NLT

How precious is Your lovingkindness, O God! Therefore the children of men put their trust under the shadow of Your wings.

PSALM 36:7 NKJV

I will tell of the kindnesses of the LORD, the deeds for which He is to be praised, according to all the LORD has done for us.

ISAIAH 63:7 NIV

Be kind to each other, tenderhearted, forgiving one another, just as God through Christ has forgiven you.

EPHESIANS 4:32 NLT

Praise the LORD, all you Gentiles! Laud Him, all you peoples! For His merciful kindness is great toward us, and the truth of the LORD endures forever.

PSALM 117:1-2 NKJV

When the Holy Spirit controls our lives, He will produce this kind of fruit in us: love, joy, peace, patience, kindness, goodness, faithfulness, gentleness, and self-control.

GALATIANS 5:22-23 NLT

When the kindness and love of God our Savior appeared, He saved us, not because of righteous things we had done, but because of His mercy. He saved us through the washing of rebirth and renewal by the Holy Spirit.

TITUS 3:4-5 NIV

Do not withhold Your tender mercies from me, O LORD; let Your lovingkindness and Your truth continually preserve me.

PSALM 40:11 NKJV

An anxious heart weighs a man down, but a kind word cheers him up.

PROVERBS 12:25 NIV

Your own soul is nourished when you are kind, but you destroy yourself when you are cruel.

PROVERBS 11:17 NLT

"Whoever gives one of these little ones even a cup of cold water because he is a disciple, truly, I say to you, he will by no means lose his reward."

MATTHEW 10:42 ESV

Make sure that nobody pays back wrong for wrong, but always try to be kind to each other and to everyone else.

1 THESSALONIANS 5:15 NIV

Patience

Those who wait on the LORD shall renew their strength; they shall mount up with wings like eagles, they shall run and not be weary, they shall walk and not faint.

ISAIAH 40:31 NKJV

The Lord is not slow in keeping His promise, as some understand slowness. He is patient with you, not wanting anyone to perish, but everyone to come to repentance.

2 PETER 3:9 NIV

The LORD is good to those who wait for Him, to the soul who seeks Him.

LAMENTATIONS 3:25 ESV

You, O Lord, are a God full of compassion, and gracious, longsuffering and abundant in mercy and truth.

PSALM 86:15 NKJV

Be still before the LORD and wait patiently for Him; do not fret when men succeed in their ways. Refrain from anger and turn from wrath.

PSALM 37:7-8 NIV

Patient endurance is what you need now, so you will continue to do God's will. Then you will receive all that He has promised.

HEBREWS 10:36 NLT

Hope that is seen is no hope at all. Who hopes for what he already has? But if we hope for what we do not yet have, we wait for it patiently.

ROMANS 8:24-25 NIV

I waited patiently for the LORD; and He inclined to me, and heard my cry.

PSALM 40:1 NKJV

Be glad for all God is planning for you. Be patient in trouble, and always be prayerful.

ROMANS 12:12 NLT

Whoever is slow to anger is better than the mighty, and he who rules his spirit than he who takes a city.

PROVERBS 16:32 ESV

Be humble and gentle. Be patient with each other, making allowance for each other's faults because of your love. Always keep yourselves united in the Holy Spirit, and bind yourselves together with peace.

EPHESIANS 4:2-3 NLT

Better is the end of a thing than its beginning, and the patient in spirit is better than the proud in spirit.

ECCLESIASTES 7:8 ESV

Brothers and sisters, we urge you to warn those who are lazy. Encourage those who are timid. Take tender care of those who are weak. Be patient with everyone.

1 THESSALONIANS 5:14 NLT

Peace

You will keep in perfect peace all who trust in You, whose thoughts are fixed on You!

ISAIAH 26:3 NLT

I will both lie down in peace, and sleep; for You alone, O LORD, make me dwell in safety.

PSALM 4:8 NKJV

May the Lord of peace Himself always give you His peace no matter what happens. The Lord be with you all.

2 THESSALONIANS 3:16 NLT

For He Himself is our peace, who has made the two one and has destroyed the barrier, the dividing wall of hostility, by abolishing in His flesh the law with its commandments and regulations.

EPHESIANS 2:14-15 NIV

"Blessed are the peacemakers, for they shall be called sons of God."

MATTHEW 5:9 ESV

"I am leaving you with a gift – peace of mind and heart. And the peace I give isn't like the peace the world gives. So don't be troubled or afraid."

JOHN 14:27 NLT

"Glory to God in the highest, and on earth peace among those with whom He is pleased!"

LUKE 2:14 ESV

You are my hiding place; You protect me from trouble. You surround me with songs of victory.

PSALM 32:7 NLT

Let the peace of Christ rule in your hearts, since as members of one body you were called to peace. And be thankful.

COLOSSIANS 3:15 NIV

Those who love Your law have great peace and do not stumble.

PSALM 119:165 NLT

Make every effort to keep the unity of the Spirit through the bond of peace.

EPHESIANS 4:3 NIV

A dry crust eaten in peace is better than a great feast with strife.

PROVERBS 17:1 NLT

Grace to you and peace from God our Father and the Lord Jesus Christ.

ROMANS 1:7 ESV

Pursue faith and love and peace, and enjoy the companionship of those who call on the Lord with pure hearts.

2 TIMOTHY 2:22 NLT

*P*erseverance

Blessed is the man who endures temptation; for when he has been approved, he will receive the crown of life which the Lord has promised to those who love Him.

JAMES 1:12 NKJV

"All who are victorious will inherit all these blessings, and I will be their God, and they will be My children."

REVELATION 21:7 NLT

Be steadfast, immovable, always abounding in the work of the Lord, knowing that in the Lord your labor is not in vain.

1 CORINTHIANS 15:58 ESV

Let us not grow weary while doing good, for in due season we shall reap if we do not lose heart.

GALATIANS 6:9 NKJV

"The one who endures to the end will be saved."

MATTHEW 24:13 ESV

We also rejoice in our sufferings, because we know that suffering produces perseverance; perseverance, character; and character, hope. And hope does not disappoint us, because God has poured out His love into our hearts by the Holy Spirit, whom He has given us.

ROMANS 5:3-5 NIV

Be strong and do not let your hands be weak, for your work shall be rewarded!

2 CHRONICLES 15:7 NKJV

Consider it pure joy, my brothers, whenever you face trials of many kinds, because you know that the testing of your faith develops perseverance. Perseverance must finish its work so that you may be mature and complete, not lacking anything.

JAMES 1:2-4 NIV

"Because you have obeyed My command to persevere, I will protect you from the great time of testing that will come upon the whole world to test those who belong to this world."

REVELATION 3:10 NLT

Let us throw off everything that hinders and the sin that so easily entangles, and let us run with perseverance the race marked out for us.

HEBREWS 12:1 NIV

For we share in Christ, if indeed we hold our original confidence firm to the end.

HEBREWS 3:14 ESV

"Everyone will hate you because of your allegiance to Me. But those who endure to the end will be saved."

MATTHEW 10:22 NLT

Prayer

The earnest prayer of a righteous person has great power and wonderful results.

JAMES 5:16 NLT

"It shall come to pass that before they call, I will answer; and while they are still speaking, I will hear."

ISAIAH 65:24 NKJV

The LORD is near to all who call on Him, to all who call on Him in truth. He fulfills the desires of those who fear Him; He hears their cry and saves them.

PSALM 145:18-19 NIV

"Truly, truly, I say to you, whatever you ask of the Father in My name, He will give it to you. Until now you have asked nothing in My name. Ask, and you will receive, that your joy may be full."

JOHN 16:23-24 ESV

Be anxious for nothing, but in everything by prayer and supplication, with thanksgiving, let your requests be made known to God; and the peace of God, which surpasses all understanding, will guard your hearts and minds through Christ Jesus.

PHILIPPIANS 4:6-7 NKJV

"When you pray, go into your room, close the door and pray to your Father, who is unseen. Then your Father, who sees what is done in secret, will reward you."

MATTHEW 6:6 NIV

"Whatever you ask in prayer, you will receive, if you have faith."

MATTHEW 21:22 ESV

While Jesus was here on earth, He offered prayers and pleadings, with a loud cry and tears, to the One who could deliver Him out of death. And God heard His prayers because of His reverence for God.

HEBREWS 5:7 NLT

"I say to you, whatever things you ask when you pray, believe that you receive them, and you will have them."

MARK 11:24 NKJV

"Call upon Me in the day of trouble; I will deliver you, and you will honor Me."

PSALM 50:15 NIV

"In those days when you pray, I will listen. If you look for Me in earnest, you will find Me when you seek Me."

JEREMIAH 29:12-13 NLT

For the eyes of the Lord are on the righteous and His ears are attentive to their prayer.

1 PETER 3:12 NIV

Protection

The Lord is faithful, and He will strengthen and protect you from the evil one.

2 THESSALONIANS 3:3 NIV

He who dwells in the secret place of the Most High shall abide under the shadow of the Almighty. I will say of the LORD, "He is my refuge and my fortress; my God, in Him I will trust."

PSALM 91:1-2 NKJV

We know that those who have become part of God's family do not make a practice of sinning, for God's Son holds them securely, and the evil one cannot get his hands on them.

1 JOHN 5:18 NLT

The LORD preserves the simple; I was brought low, and He saved me.

PSALM 116:6 NKJV

How great is Your goodness, which You have stored up for those who fear You, which You bestow in the sight of men on those who take refuge in You.

PSALM 31:19 NIV

"The beloved of the LORD dwells in safety. The High God surrounds him all day long, and dwells between his shoulders."

DEUTERONOMY 33:12 ESV

The angel of the LORD guards all who fear Him, and He rescues them.

PSALM 34:7 NLT

When you lie down, you will not be afraid; when you lie down, your sleep will be sweet.

PROVERBS 3:24 NIV

For the LORD orders His angels to protect you wherever you go.

PSALM 91:11 NLT

The LORD is my light and my salvation; whom shall I fear? The LORD is the strength of my life; of whom shall I be afraid?

PSALM 27:1-2 NKJV

The name of the LORD is a strong tower; the righteous man runs into it and is safe.

PROVERBS 18:10 ESV

The LORD keeps you from all evil and preserves your life. The LORD keeps watch over you as you come and go, both now and forever.

PSALM 121:7-8 NLT

Let all who take refuge in You be glad; let them ever sing for joy. Spread Your protection over them, that those who love Your name may rejoice in You.

PSALM 5:11 NIV

Provision

The LORD bestows favor and honor. No good thing does He withhold from those who walk uprightly.

PSALM 84:11 ESV

God is able to make all grace abound to you, so that in all things at all times, having all that you need, you will abound in every good work.

2 CORINTHIANS 9:8 NIV

Jesus said to them, "I am the bread of life, whoever comes to Me shall not hunger, and whoever believes in Me shall never thirst."

JOHN 6:35 ESV

"Your Father knows the things you have need of before you ask Him."

MATTHEW 6:8 NKJV

His divine power has granted to us all things that pertain to life and godliness, through the knowledge of Him who called us to His own glory and excellence.

2 PETER 1:3 ESV

Even when we were with you, we gave you this rule: "If a man will not work, he shall not eat."

2 THESSALONIANS 3:10 NIV

Don't forget to do good and to share what you have with those in need, for such sacrifices are very pleasing to God.

HEBREWS 13:16 NLT

He will give grass in your fields for your livestock, and you shall eat and be full.

DEUTERONOMY 11:15 ESV

The LORD is my shepherd, I shall not be in want.

PSALM 23:1 NIV

My God will meet all your needs according to His glorious riches in Christ Jesus.

PHILIPPIANS 4:19 NIV

Lazy people are soon poor; hard workers get rich. A wise youth works hard all summer; a youth who sleeps away the hour of opportunity brings shame.

PROVERBS 10:4-5 NLT

"I will raise up for them a garden of renown, and they shall no longer be consumed with hunger in the land, nor bear the shame of the Gentiles anymore. Thus they shall know that I, the LORD their God, am with them."

EZEKIEL 34:29-30 NKJV

Respect

Pay to all what is owed to them: taxes to whom taxes are owed, revenue to whom revenue is owed, respect to whom respect is owed, honor to whom honor is owed.

ROMANS 13:7 ESV

You, dear friends, must continue to build your lives on the foundation of your holy faith.

JUDE 20 NLT

Do nothing out of selfish ambition or vain conceit, but in humility consider others better than yourselves.

PHILIPPIANS 2:3 NIV

You are worthy, O Lord our God, to receive glory and honor and power. For You created everything.

REVELATION 4:11 NLT

Let each one of you love his wife as himself, and let the wife see that she respects her husband.

EPHESIANS 5:33 ESV

Honor your father and your mother, so that you may live long in the land the LORD your God is giving you.

EXODUS 20:12 NIV

"For whoever exalts himself will be humbled, and he who humbles himself will be exalted."

LUKE 14:11 NKJV

Glory and honor and peace for everyone who does good.

ROMANS 2:10 ESV

Blessed is that man who makes the LORD his trust, and does not respect the proud, nor such as turn aside to lies.

PSALM 40:4 NKJV

Honor those who are your leaders in the Lord's work.

1 THESSALONIANS 5:12 NLT

Hold me up, and I shall be safe, and I shall observe Your statutes continually.

PSALM 119:117 NKJV

Show proper respect to everyone: Love the brotherhood of believers.

1 PETER 2:17 NIV

This should be your ambition: to live a quiet life, minding your own business and working with your hands. As a result, people who are not Christians will respect the way you live.

1 THESSALONIANS 4:11-12 NLT

Rest

"Come to Me, all you who are weary and burdened, and I will give you rest. Take My yoke upon you and learn from Me, for I am gentle and humble in heart, and you will find rest for your souls."

MATTHEW 11:28-29 NIV

All who enter into God's rest will find rest from their labors, just as God rested after creating the world.

HEBREWS 4:10 NLT

"In returning and rest you shall be saved; in quietness and in trust shall be your strength."

ISAIAH 30:15 ESV

My people will live in safety, quietly at home. They will be at rest.

ISAIAH 32:18 NLT

"My Presence will go with you, and I will give you rest."

EXODUS 33:14 NKJV

The fear of the LORD leads to life, and whoever has it rests satisfied; he will not be visited by harm.

PROVERBS 19:23 ESV

[The LORD] lets me rest in green meadows; He leads me beside peaceful streams. He renews my strength.

PSALM 23:2-3 NLT

I will lie down and sleep in peace, for You alone, O LORD, make me dwell in safety.

PSALM 4:8 NIV

"Remember to observe the Sabbath day by keeping it holy. Six days a week are set apart for your daily duties and regular work, but the seventh day is a day of rest dedicated to the LORD your God."

EXODUS 20:8-10 NLT

My soul finds rest in God alone; my salvation comes from Him. He alone is my rock and my salvation; He is my fortress, I will never be shaken.

PSALM 62:1-2 NIV

The LORD your God in your midst, the Mighty One, will save; He will rejoice over you with gladness, He will quiet you with His love, He will rejoice over you with singing.

ZEPHANIAH 3:17 NKJV

"I will refresh the weary and satisfy the faint."

JEREMIAH 31:25 NIV

Return to your rest, O my soul, for the LORD has dealt bountifully with you.

PSALM 116:7 NKJV

Satisfaction

Delight yourself also in the LORD, and He shall give you the desires of your heart.

PSALM 37:4 NKJV

Keep your lives free from the love of money and be content with what you have, because God has said, "Never will I leave you; never will I forsake you."

HEBREWS 13:5 NIV

Satisfy us in the morning with Your steadfast love, that we may rejoice and be glad all our days.

PSALM 90:14 ESV

Command those who are rich in this present age not to be haughty, nor to trust in uncertain riches but in the living God, who gives us richly all things to enjoy.

1 TIMOTHY 6:17 NKJV

You open Your hand and satisfy the desires of every living thing.

PSALM 145:16 NIV

True religion with contentment is great wealth. After all, we didn't bring anything with us when we came into the world, and we certainly cannot carry anything with us when we die. So if we have enough food and clothing, let us be content.

1 TIMOTHY 6:6-8 NLT

For the sake of Christ, then, I am content with weaknesses, insults, hardships, persecutions, and calamities. For when I am weak, then I am strong.

2 CORINTHIANS 12:10 ESV

Let them give thanks to the LORD for His unfailing love and His wonderful deeds for men, for He satisfies the thirsty and fills the hungry with good things.

PSALM 107:8-9 NIV

God blesses you who are hungry now, for you will be satisfied.

LUKE 6:21 NLT

My soul will be satisfied as with the richest of foods; with singing lips my mouth will praise You.

PSALM 63:5 NIV

"Whoever drinks of the water that I will give him will never be thirsty forever. The water that I will give him will become in him a spring of water welling up to eternal life."

JOHN 4:14 ESV

"God blesses those who are hungry and thirsty for justice, for they will receive it in full."

MATTHEW 5:6 NLT

Self-Control

Don't use foul or abusive language. Let everything you say be good and helpful, so that your words will be an encouragement to those who hear them.

EPHESIANS 4:29 NLT

Set a guard, O LORD, over my mouth; keep watch over the door of my lips!

PSALM 141:3 ESV

Follow the Lord's rules for doing His work, just as an athlete either follows the rules or is disqualified and wins no prize.

2 TIMOTHY 2:5 NLT

Every athlete exercises self-control in all things. They do it to receive a perishable wreath, but we an imperishable.

1 CORINTHIANS 9:25 ESV

A man without self-control is like a city broken into and left without walls.

PROVERBS 25:28 ESV

Those who control their tongue will have a long life; a quick retort can ruin everything.

PROVERBS 13:3 NLT

No temptation has seized you except what is common to man. And God is faithful; He will not let you be tempted beyond what you can bear. But when you are tempted, He will also provide a way out so that you can stand up under it.

1 CORINTHIANS 10:13 NIV

Knowing God leads to self-control. Self-control leads to patient endurance, and patient endurance leads to godliness.

2 PETER 1:6 NLT

A gentle answer turns away wrath, but a harsh word stirs up anger.

PROVERBS 15:1 NIV

"I tell you, on the day of judgment people will give account for every careless word they speak, for by your words you will be justified."

MATTHEW 12:36-37 ESV

When words are many, sin is not absent, but he who holds his tongue is wise.

PROVERBS 10:19 NIV

God gave us a spirit not of fear but of power and love and self-control.

2 TIMOTHY 1:7 ESV

When the Holy Spirit controls our lives, He will produce this kind of fruit in us: love, joy, peace, patience, kindness, goodness, faithfulness, gentleness, and self-control.

GALATIANS 5:22-23 NLT

Strength

I can do all things through Christ who strengthens me.

PHILIPPIANS 4:13 NKJV

God gives power to the faint, and to him who has no might He increases strength.

ISAIAH 40:29 ESV

"My gracious favor is all you need. My power works best in your weakness." So now I am glad to boast about my weaknesses, so that the power of Christ may work through me.

2 CORINTHIANS 12:9 NLT

I pray also that the eyes of your heart may be enlightened in order that you may know the hope to which He has called you, and His incomparably great power for us who believe.

EPHESIANS 1:18-19 NIV

"Do not fear, for I am with you; do not be dismayed, for I am your God. I will strengthen you and help you; I will uphold you with My righteous right hand."

ISAIAH 41:10 NIV

God is my strength and power, and He makes my way perfect. He makes my feet like the feet of deer, and sets me on my high places.

2 SAMUEL 22:33-34 NKJV

The LORD is my strength and my song, and He has become my salvation.

EXODUS 15:2 ESV

The LORD gives strength to His people; the LORD blesses His people with peace.

PSALM 29:11 NIV

The LORD is my strength and my shield; my heart trusted in Him, and I am helped.

PSALM 28:7 NKJV

My health may fail, and my spirit may grow weak, but God remains the strength of my heart; He is mine forever.

PSALM 73:26 NLT

God is our refuge and strength, an ever-present help in trouble.

PSALM 46:1 NIV

Praise and glory and wisdom and thanks and honor and strength be to our God for ever and ever. Amen.

REVELATION 7:12 NIV

The joy of the LORD is your strength.

NEHEMIAH 8:10 ESV

Success

May [the LORD] give you the desire of your heart and make all your plans succeed.

PSALM 20:4 NIV

The reward for humility and fear of the LORD is riches and honor and life.

PROVERBS 22:4 ESV

Believe in the LORD your God, and you will be able to stand firm.

2 CHRONICLES 20:20 NLT

"For I know the thoughts that I think toward you," says the LORD, "thoughts of peace and not of evil, to give you a future and a hope."

JEREMIAH 29:11 NKJV

Hard work means prosperity; only fools idle away their time.

PROVERBS 12:11 NLT

In the morning sow your seed, and in the evening do not withhold your hand; for you do not know which will prosper, either this or that, or whether both alike will be good.

ECCLESIASTES 11:6 NKJV

It is not that we think we can do anything of lasting value by ourselves. Our only power and success come from God.

2 CORINTHIANS 3:5 NLT

Remember me, O LORD, when You show favor to Your people, come to my aid when You save them, that I may enjoy the prosperity of Your chosen ones, that I may share in the joy of Your nation and join Your inheritance in giving praise.

PSALM 106:4-5 NIV

This Book of the Law shall not depart from your mouth, but you shall meditate in it day and night. For then you will make your way prosperous, and then you will have good success.

JOSHUA 1:8 NKJV

Commit to the LORD whatever you do, and your plans will succeed.

PROVERBS 16:3 NIV

With God's help we will do mighty things, for He will trample down our foes.

PSALM 60:12 NLT

He who trusts in the LORD will prosper.

PROVERBS 28:25 NIV

It is possible to give freely and become more wealthy, but those who are stingy will lose everything. The generous prosper and are satisfied; those who refresh others will themselves be refreshed.

PROVERBS 11:24-25 NLT

I walk in the way of righteousness, in the paths of justice, granting an inheritance to those who love me, and filling their treasuries.

PROVERBS 8:20-21 ESV

Teamwork

Let us not give up meeting together, as some are in the habit of doing, but let us encourage one another – and all the more as you see the Day approaching.

HEBREWS 10:25 NIV

Share each other's troubles and problems, and in this way obey the law of Christ.

GALATIANS 6:2 NLT

Finally, all of you, live in harmony with one another; be sympathetic, love as brothers, be compassionate and humble.

1 PETER 3:8 NIV

Two are better than one, because they have a good reward for their toil. For if they fall, one will lift up his fellow.

ECCLESIASTES 4:9-10 ESV

"A new commandment I give to you, that you love one another; as I have loved you, that you also love one another."

JOHN 13:34 NKJV

The people all responded together, "We will do everything the LORD has said."

EXODUS 19:8 NIV

Now may the God of patience and comfort grant you to be like-minded toward one another, according to Christ Jesus, that you may with one mind and one mouth glorify the God and Father of our Lord Jesus Christ.

ROMANS 15:5-6 NKJV

Come, let us tell of the LORD's greatness; let us exalt His name together.

PSALM 34:3 NLT

A friend loves at all times, and a brother is born for adversity.

PROVERBS 17:17 NIV

As iron sharpens iron, a friend sharpens a friend.

PROVERBS 27:17 NLT

"Where two or three come together in My name, there am I with them."

MATTHEW 18:20 NIV

Love each other with genuine affection, and take delight in honoring each other.

ROMANS 12:10 NLT

Be of the same mind toward one another. Do not set your mind on high things, but associate with the humble.

ROMANS 12:16 NKJV

Do not forget to do good and to share with others, for with such sacrifices God is pleased.

HEBREWS 13:16 NIV

Thankfulness

Give thanks to the LORD, for He is good! His faithful love endures forever.

1 CHRONICLES 16:34 NLT

Continue earnestly in prayer, being vigilant in it with thanksgiving.

COLOSSIANS 4:2 NKJV

The LORD has done great things for us, and we are filled with joy.

PSALM 126:3 NIV

Always give thanks for everything to God the Father in the name of our Lord Jesus Christ.

EPHESIANS 5:20 NLT

Praise the Lord! I will give thanks to the LORD with my whole heart. Great are the works of the LORD, studied by all who delight in them.

PSALM 111:1-2 ESV

Give thanks to the LORD, call on His name; make known among the nations what He has done. Sing to Him, sing praise to Him; tell of all His wonderful acts.

1 CHRONICLES 16:8-9 NIV

In everything give thanks; for this is the will of God in Christ Jesus for you.

1 THESSALONIANS 5:18 NKJV

O LORD, You are my God; I will exalt You and praise Your name, for in perfect faithfulness You have done marvelous things.

ISAIAH 25:1 NIV

Oh, taste and see that the LORD is good! Blessed is the man who takes refuge in Him!

PSALM 34:8 ESV

We give thanks to You, O God; we give thanks, for Your name is near.

PSALM 75:1 NIV

May the words of my mouth and the thoughts of my heart be pleasing to You, O Lord, my rock and my redeemer.

PSALM 19:14 NLT

Enter into His gates with thanksgiving, and into His courts with praise. Be thankful to Him, and bless His name.

PSALM 100:4 NKJV

Let your lives overflow with thanksgiving for all He has done.

COLOSSIANS 2:7 NLT

I will give thanks to the Lord because of His righteousness and will sing praise to the name of the Lord Most High.

PSALM 7:17 NIV

Trust

Those who know Your name will trust in You, for You, LORD, have never forsaken those who seek You.

PSALM 9:10 NIV

Let us hold fast the confession of our hope without wavering, for He who promised is faithful.

HEBREWS 10:23 ESV

For to this end we both labor and suffer reproach, because we trust in the living God, who is the Savior of all men, especially of those who believe.

1 TIMOTHY 4:10 NKJV

I trust in God, so why should I be afraid? What can mere mortals do to me?

PSALM 56:11 NLT

"Surely this is our God; we trusted in Him, and He saved us. This is the LORD, we trusted in Him; let us rejoice and be glad in His salvation."

ISAIAH 25:9 NIV

Behold, God is my salvation; I will trust, and will not be afraid; for the LORD GOD is my strength and my song, and He has become my salvation.

ISAIAH 12:2 ESV

Trust in Him at all times, you people; pour out your heart before Him; God is a refuge for us.

PSALM 62:8 NKJV

"See, I lay a stone in Zion, a chosen and precious cornerstone, and the one who trusts in Him will never be put to shame."

1 PETER 2:6 NIV

The LORD is good. When trouble comes, He is a strong refuge. And He knows everyone who trusts in Him.

NAHUM 1:7 NLT

Blessed are all those who put their trust in Him.

PSALM 2:12 NKJV

May the God of hope fill you with all joy and peace as you trust in Him, so that you may overflow with hope by the power of the Holy Spirit.

ROMANS 15:13 NIV

Trust in the LORD with all your heart, and lean not on your own understanding; in all your ways acknowledge Him, and He shall direct your paths.

PROVERBS 3:5-6 NKJV

In Him our hearts rejoice, for we are trusting in His holy name.

PSALM 33:21 NLT

Wisdom

Oh, the depth of the riches of the wisdom and knowledge of God! How unsearchable His judgments, and His paths beyond tracing out!

ROMANS 11:33 NIV

The wisdom from above is first pure, then peaceable, gentle, open to reason, full of mercy and good fruits, impartial and sincere. And a harvest of righteousness is sown in peace by those who make peace.

JAMES 3:17-18 ESV

The LORD gives wisdom, and from His mouth come knowledge and understanding.

PROVERBS 2:6 NIV

If you need wisdom – if you want to know what God wants you to do – ask Him, and He will gladly tell you. He will not resent your asking.

JAMES 1:5 NLT

To the man who pleases Him, God gives wisdom, knowledge and happiness.

ECCLESIASTES 2:26 NIV

Wisdom is sweet to your soul. If you find it, you will have a bright future, and your hopes will not be cut short.

PROVERBS 24:14 NLT

The fruit of the righteous is a tree of life, and he who wins souls is wise.

PROVERBS 11:30 NIV

The fear of the LORD is the beginning of wisdom; a good understanding have all those who do His commandments. His praise endures forever.

PSALM 111:10 NKJV

Happy is the person who finds wisdom and gains understanding. For the profit of wisdom is better than silver, and her wages are better than gold.

PROVERBS 3:13-14 NLT

Wisdom strengthens the wise more than ten rulers of the city.

ECCLESIASTES 7:19 NKJV

Learn to be wise, and develop good judgment. Don't turn your back on wisdom, for she will protect you.

PROVERBS 4:5-6 NLT

Wisdom and knowledge will be the stability of your times, and the strength of salvation; the fear of the LORD is His treasure.

ISAIAH 33:6 NKJV

Fear of the LORD is the beginning of wisdom. Knowledge of the Holy One results in understanding.

PROVERBS 9:10 NLT